WEATHER

A Follett Beginning SCIENCE Book

SCIENCE EDUCATION CONSULTANTS

EDWARD VICTOR, Ed.D.
PROFESSOR OF SCIENCE EDUCATION
NORTHWESTERN UNIVERSITY

CURTIS MELNICK, Ed.D.
DISTRICT SUPERINTENDENT OF SCHOOLS
CHICAGO PUBLIC SCHOOLS

READING CONSULTANT

JEANNE S. BROUILLETTE
CURRICULUM COORDINATOR
EVANSTON ELEMENTARY SCHOOLS

TECHNICAL CONSULTANT

IVAN W. BRUNK
SUPERVISING PUBLIC SERVICE METEOROLOGIST
UNITED STATES WEATHER BUREAU
CHICAGO, ILLINOIS

TESTED IN THE EVANSTON PUBLIC SCHOOLS

WEATHER

Julian May

Illustrated by Jack White
Cover illustration by Alex Ebel

Follett Publishing Company   Chicago · New York

   Library of Congress Catalog Card Number: 66-10049

SBN 695-49210-1 Titan binding   SBN 695-89210-X Trade binding   Second Printing

A weather report tells us about the air outdoors. It tells us if it is hot or cold, windy or calm, wet or dry, cloudy or clear.

Our planet earth has weather because it has air. The science of the air and its weather is called meteorology.

Weather keeps changing. It changes
hour by hour and day by day. Weather and
climate in one part of the world are not
the same as they are in another place.

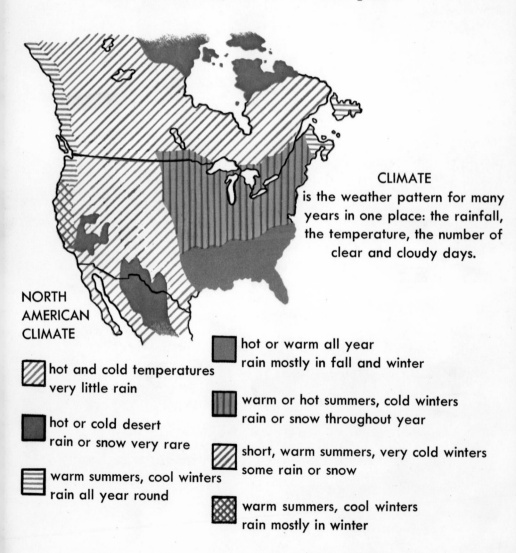

CLIMATE
is the weather pattern for many
years in one place: the rainfall,
the temperature, the number of
clear and cloudy days.

NORTH
AMERICAN
CLIMATE

hot and cold temperatures
very little rain

hot or cold desert
rain or snow very rare

warm summers, cool winters
rain all year round

hot or warm all year
rain mostly in fall and winter

warm or hot summers, cold winters
rain or snow throughout year

short, warm summers, very cold winters
some rain or snow

warm summers, cool winters
rain mostly in winter

The earth's blanket of air is called the atmosphere. It has layers. Most of the earth's weather happens in the bottom layer of atmosphere, called the troposphere. A little bit of weather happens in the lower part of the stratosphere.

STRATOSPHERE
about 10 to 50 miles up

some thundercloud tops are more than 10 miles high

TROPOSPHERE
surface to 5 to 10 miles up

most clouds are less than 5 miles high

highest mountain 5½ miles high

THE ATMOSPHERE'S BOTTOM LAYERS

The great weather-maker for the earth is the sun. The heat energy of the sun acts on the air, the land, and the water to make different kinds of weather.

AIR
- heats faster than water or land
- rises when heated, sinks when cooled
- gets heat from the sun
- is heated and cooled by land and water

LAND
- heats and cools slower than air
- heats and cools faster than water
- holds heat it gets from the sun
- heats or cools air moving over it

WATER
- heats and cools slower than air and land
- heats or cools air moving over it
- changes from solid to liquid to gas as it is heated

Weather scientists want to know how hot or how cold the air is. The hotness or the coldness of something is called its temperature. The thermometers in the picture are used to tell the temperature of the air.

Air is mostly heated or cooled by the land that it moves over. The air can also be heated or cooled when it passes over the sea. The sun also heats the air, but it does not heat it as well as land or water does.

THERMOMETERS

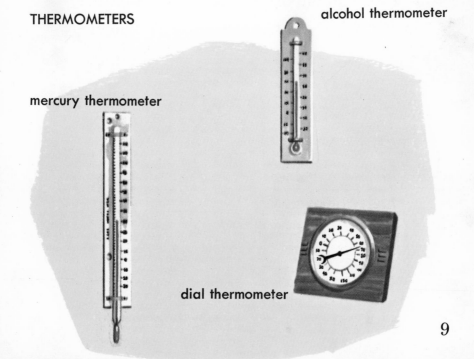

alcohol thermometer

mercury thermometer

dial thermometer

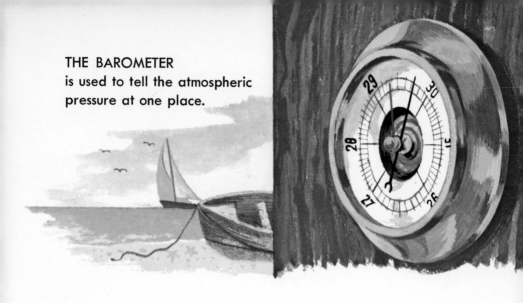

THE BAROMETER
is used to tell the atmospheric
pressure at one place.

Air has pressure. The pressure of the
air is also an important part of the weather
report. We do not feel the pressure when the
air is not moving. But when the wind blows,
we know that the air has pressure because we
feel it pushing us.

Air pressure, or atmospheric pressure, is
not the same through the whole air blanket.
Air high above the earth has less pressure than
air nearer the earth. Cold air at one height
has more pressure than warm air at the same
height.

When air moves, it often moves in a big body hundreds of miles wide, called an air mass. Some air masses are cool. Others are warm.

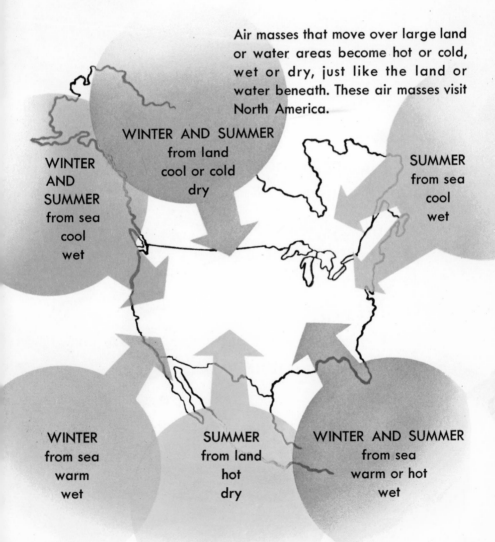

Air masses that move over large land or water areas become hot or cold, wet or dry, just like the land or water beneath. These air masses visit North America.

WINTER AND SUMMER
from land
cool or cold
dry

WINTER
AND
SUMMER
from sea
cool
wet

SUMMER
from sea
cool
wet

WINTER
from sea
warm
wet

SUMMER
from land
hot
dry

WINTER AND SUMMER
from sea
warm or hot
wet

A COLD AIR MASS
seen as if it were cut in half.
The darker center has the highest
pressure. Air flows downward
and outward from the center.

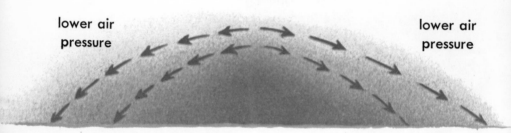

high air
pressure

lower air
pressure

lower air
pressure

When a cold air mass meets a warm air
mass, they do not usually mix. They stay
separate.

Cold and warm air masses move across
North America. They bring different kinds
of weather with them.

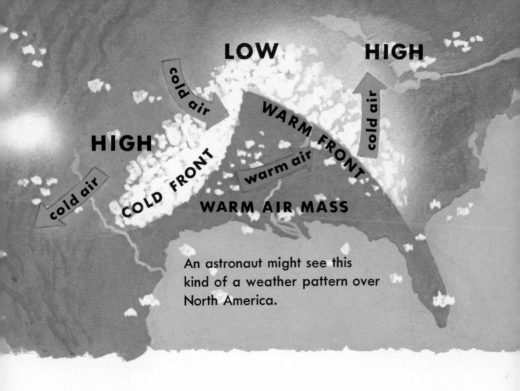

LOW   HIGH

cold air

HIGH

WARM FRONT

cold air

COLD FRONT

warm air

cold air

WARM AIR MASS

An astronaut might see this
kind of a weather pattern over
North America.

The border where a cold air mass meets
a warm air mass is called a front. A cold
front forms when a cold air mass meets and
pushes a warmer air mass. A warm front
forms when a warm air mass meets and takes
the place of a cooler air mass.

An air mass with high atmospheric
pressure at the center is called a HIGH.
Many air masses have a HIGH at the center.

Sometimes an area of low atmospheric pressure forms along a front in between a cool and a warm HIGH. This area is called a LOW. It may move along over land and water for a long way. A LOW often brings rain or snow.

A hurricane or typhoon is a very strong LOW that forms over warm seas. It has very powerful winds that can cause great damage.

A LOW
is something like a "hole" in between two air masses with higher atmospheric pressure. Winds blow counterclockwise around a LOW. They blow clockwise around a HIGH.

cold HIGH

LOW

warm HIGH

A hurricane LOW has winds that may blow more than 100 miles per hour.

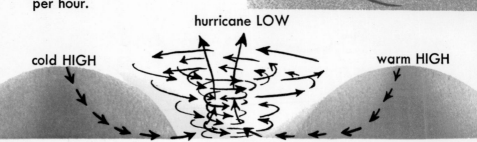

hurricane LOW

cold HIGH

warm HIGH

Wind is moving air that we can feel.
Sometimes the strength and direction of the
wind can tell us how air masses are moving.

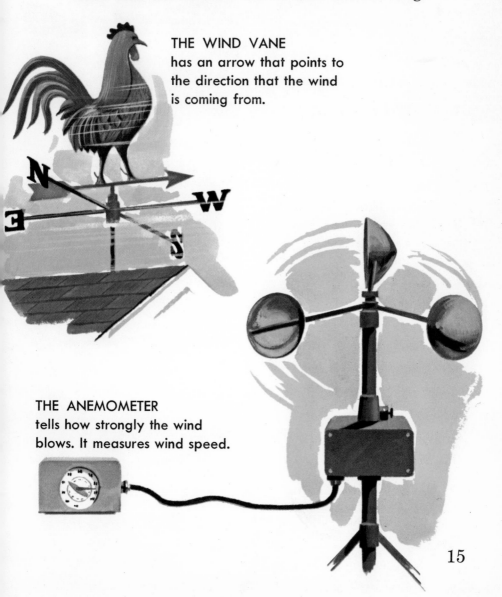

THE WIND VANE
has an arrow that points to
the direction that the wind
is coming from.

THE ANEMOMETER
tells how strongly the wind
blows. It measures wind speed.

Tornadoes grow from baggy-looking dark storm clouds.

A tornado that does not touch the ground is called a funnel cloud.

Great damage happens when a tornado touches the ground.

Tornadoes have the strongest winds on earth. Sometimes a tornado is only a few hundred feet wide. Its winds go round and round. They may go as fast as 500 miles an hour.

Water is an important part of weather. Water may be a solid, a liquid, or a gas — depending on how much heat it has. Ice and snow cover cold parts of the earth. Liquid water covers about three-quarters of the earth. Liquid water is always changing to a gas, or evaporating, at the place where it meets the air. The gas form of water is called water vapor.

WATER HAS THREE FORMS

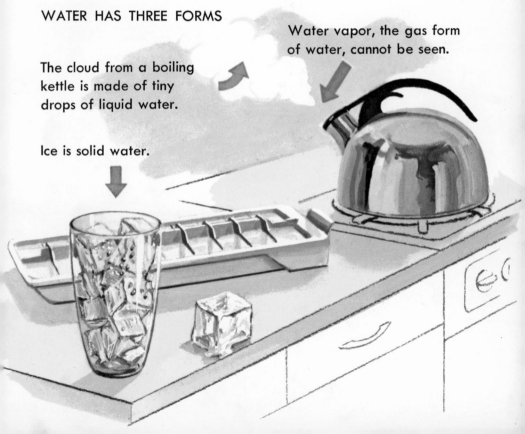

Water vapor, the gas form of water, cannot be seen.

The cloud from a boiling kettle is made of tiny drops of liquid water.

Ice is solid water.

The picture shows the movement of water that goes on in the air, on the ground, and under the ground.

THE WATER CYCLE

2 As it is cooled, water vapor turns into tiny droplets and makes clouds.

3 Water falls from clouds as rain or snow.

1 Water from lake or sea, or from green plants, changes to vapor and rises in the air.

4 Some water is taken up by green plants and given off again as vapor.

5 Some water wets the land, then turns into vapor as the land dries.

6 Some water runs on top of the land or underground until it returns to the sea or lake.

Heat and humidity together make us uncomfortable in the summertime. When the weather report tells us that the THI, or Temperature-Humidity Index, is over 70, we know we can expect an uncomfortable day.

Humidity is how much water vapor there is in the air in one place at one time. We cannot see the water vapor in the air, but our bodies can feel it. On warm days with much humidity, we feel sticky. On days when the humidity is low, our skins feel dry and tight.

Air does not always have the same humidity. Warm air can hold more water vapor in it than cold air.

These instruments tell the
relative humidity

home hygrometer

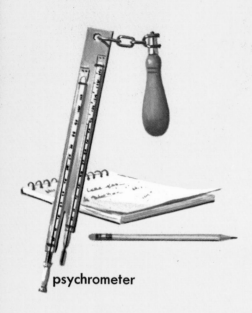

psychrometer

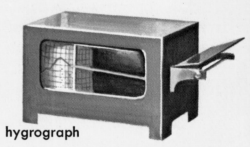

hygrograph

If the air is so full of water vapor that
it cannot hold any more, the weather report
says, "The relative humidity is 100 per cent."
If the air has only half as much water vapor
as it can hold, the report says, "The relative
humidity is 50 per cent."

When warm, wet air is chilled by resting on the cold ground, some of its water vapor changes to liquid. The water that comes out of the air sticks to the ground or the grass. These tiny drops of water are called dew. Dew does not fall like rain does. It appears in the same way that water drops appear on the outside of a glass filled with ice cubes. Frost will be formed instead of dew when the temperature is 32 degrees or lower.

Changing water vapor to liquid water

A jar filled with ice chills the air around it. Cold air cannot hold as much water vapor as warm air. Some of the invisible water vapor changes into water drops we can see.

Cumulus clouds form when warm, moist air rises very rapidly and is cooled.

Cirrus clouds are very high. They are made of tiny bits of ice.

Stratus clouds form near the ground. Fog is like a stratus cloud that touches the ground.

If invisible water vapor in the air is cooled enough, a cloud forms. You can see this happen when your warm, moist breath meets cold winter air and forms a little cloud. Large clouds in the sky are formed in somewhat the same way.

When water vapor changes into liquid water, it is said to condense. Most clouds are made of water vapor that has condensed into tiny liquid drops. But very high clouds are made of tiny bits of ice.

Sometimes rain falls from clouds. Scientists do not fully understand what makes it rain. In some way, the tiny drops in a cloud begin to come together. They gather into bigger and bigger drops. When the drops become too heavy to float in the air, they fall as rain.

The pictures show some kinds of rain clouds you might see.

Nimbostratus is a common cloud that usually has rain or snow falling from it.

Cumulonimbus, or thunderhead, causes short, powerful storms, mostly in summer.

Stratus clouds sometimes have drizzle, or light rain, falling from them.

No two snowflakes are
ever alike.

Snow is not just frozen rain. When
clouds are cooled to a very low temperature,
snow may form. Ice begins to grow around
invisible specks of dust that always float in
the air. The ice grows and grows until it
forms a small six-sided flake that we can see.
Sometimes many snowflakes stick together
before they finally fall.

Crack open a hailstone. You will find that it has layers of white and clear ice.

Water that falls from the sky in the form of rain or snow is called precipitation. The kind of precipitation called sleet is rain that passes through very cold air and freezes on the way down. Hail is another kind of precipitation. It is formed in thunderclouds when frozen rain is kept from falling by the strong winds inside the cloud. The pieces of ice grow larger and larger as they are tossed up and down. Sometimes hailstones are as big as baseballs.

25

Some storms have thunder and lightning.
Lightning is a very large electric spark. It
is caused when raindrops and tiny bits of ice
build up electric charges when they break up
inside a cloud. Lightning heats the air
quickly and makes it rush apart. The fast
movement of the air causes the loud noise
that we call thunder.

Lightning often flashes from
a cloud to the ground. It can
also go from the ground to a
cloud, or from one part of a
cloud to another part.

These clouds sometimes predict rain within 24 hours. Sailors thought the clouds looked like the pattern of a fish. They said: "Mackerel sky—rain by and by."

Atlantic mackerel

People have always wanted to know what the coming weather would be. Long ago, men began to find out that they could sometimes predict the weather, or tell it in advance, by watching for signs in nature. The picture shows a sign that is sometimes true.

Today most people depend on weather reports instead of looking for weather signs.

Weather satellites take pictures of clouds and send them by radio to scientists below.

Balloons sail high into the air and give news of air pressure, temperature, wind speed and direction, and humidity.

More than 2,000 large weather stations all over the world report weather news.

Electronic computers put together weather reports from all over and help predict coming weather.

All the world's weather scientists work together to predict or forecast the weather. Weather stations all over the earth share weather reports, because the weather moves from one place to another.

In North America, much of the weather moves from west to east.

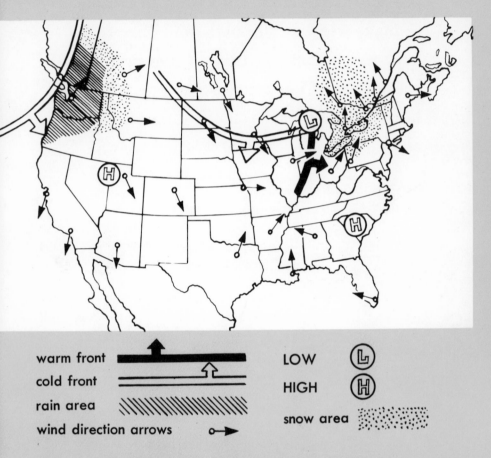

warm front	▬▲▬	LOW	Ⓛ
cold front	═══	HIGH	Ⓗ
rain area	∖∖∖∖∖∖∖		
wind direction arrows	o→	snow area	⋯⋯

Weathermen use the news they get to make a weather map. The map shows many people what the weather will be in the place where they live.

Scientists would like to do more than predict the weather. They want to be able to make weather. Farmers would like to have rain during dry times. Cities near the sea would like scientists to break up hurricanes. Perhaps some day we will be able to make the kind of weather we want.

Sprinkling clouds with chemicals sometimes makes rain or snow fall.

Words Younger Children May Need Help With

(Numbers refer to page on which the word first appears.)

5	meteorology		height		evaporating
7	atmosphere	14	area	19	humidity
	troposphere		hurricane	20	relative
	stratosphere		typhoon	22	invisible
9	scientists	15	strength		condense
	temperature		direction	25	precipitation
	thermometers	16	tornadoes		hailstones
10	pressure	17	liquid	27	predict
	atmospheric		quarters	29	forecast

THINGS TO DO IN SCHOOL OR AT HOME

Learn how to use a barometer. A barometer has two pointers. One pointer keeps moving as the atmospheric pressure changes and points to a number on the dial which tells what the pressure is. The second pointer moves only when you turn it. You set this pointer so that it lines up exactly with the first pointer. Then, when you look at the barometer later, you will be able to tell if the atmospheric pressure is rising or falling. Tap the barometer gently with one finger before you read it. Rising pressure usually means fair weather is coming. Falling pressure sometimes means that stormy weather is on its way.

Read the Follett Beginning Science Book, AIR, to learn more about the layers of the atmosphere, the make-up of air, air pressure, and winds.

Set up a weather station. Set up your own weather station. You can build many of the instruments yourself. There are many books in the library that will show you how. You will need a thermometer to find the temperature, a barometer to find air pressure, a wind vane to find the direction of the wind, an anemometer to find wind speed, a hygrometer to find relative humidity, and a rain gauge to find how much rain has fallen. You can get weather maps from your local newspaper or weather bureau.

Keep a record of the weather. Keep a daily weather chart for a month. Make seven columns on a sheet of paper. In the first column write the date and time you make your record. You should try to make your record the same time each day. In the other six columns write down the temperature outdoors, the atmospheric pressure, the humidity, the direction and speed of the wind, the condition of the sky, and the kind of precipitation (if any) and how much has fallen. In the column telling about the condition of the sky, tell how much of the sky is covered with clouds by blacking in a whole circle, part of the circle, or none of the circle. The more of the circle that you blacken, the more the sky is covered with clouds. While you are keeping this record of the weather, cut out the weather forecast from the newspaper each day. Compare the weather you found for each day with the weather that was predicted. See how often the weatherman was correct.

Examine snow crystals. If it should snow outside, catch some snowflakes on a soft, dark cloth. Try to catch single snow crystals, not big partly melted flakes. Look at the crystals through a magnifying glass. Snowflakes have six sides. A few have three sides. See if you can find any that are alike.